CA$H IN ON
YOUR SKILLS

WAYS TO MAKE MONEY WORKING OUTSIDE

CHARLOTTE TAYLOR

Enslow Publishing
101 W. 23rd Street
Suite 240
New York, NY 10011
USA

enslow.com

Published in 2020 by Enslow Publishing, LLC
101 W. 23rd Street, Suite 240, New York, NY 10011

Library of Congress Cataloging-in-Publication Data

Names: Taylor, Charlotte, author.
Title: Ways to make money working outside / Charlotte Taylor.
Description: New York: Enslow Publishing, 2020. | Series: Cash in on your skills |
Includes bibliographical references and index. | Audience: Grades 7–12.
Identifiers: LCCN 2019013437| ISBN 9781978515499 (library bound) | ISBN
 9781978515482 (pbk.)
Subjects: LCSH: Vocational guidance—Juvenile literature. | Outdoor life—Juvenile
literature.
Classification: LCC HF5381.2 .T39 2020 | DDC 331.702—dc23
LC record available at https://lccn.loc.gov/2019013437

Printed in China

Portions of this book originally appeared in *Money–Making Opportunities for Teens
Who Like Working Outside* by Tamra B. Orr.

CONTENTS

Introduction 4

CHAPTER ONE
Working for the Summer 7

CHAPTER TWO
You're In Charge 19

CHAPTER THREE
Outdoor Intern 34

CHAPTER FOUR
Step Up and Volunteer 42

CHAPTER FIVE
Getting Down to Business 52

CHAPTER SIX
Looking Ahead 59

GLOSSARY 69
FURTHER READING 71
BIBLIOGRAPHY 73
INDEX 78

Introduction

L ike many teenagers who live close to a lake, Emerson Asselta loved zipping around on his jet ski. But it was just something fun to do in his free time; that is, until one summer, when he got a brilliant idea.

It all started when Emerson took a job as a busboy at an inn on Bostwick Lake in Rockford, Michigan. Lots of people came to eat at the restaurant. But Emerson suspected that there were plenty more potential customers in nearby lakefront homes and even out on the water in boats. That's when it came to him: he could deliver food on his jet ski. It wasn't difficult for him to determine if there was a need for the service: "I Google searched 'jet ski pizza delivery service' and nothing popped up," he said. That was all he needed to know.

The following summer, at age sixteen, Emerson started up his delivery service. People loved the idea! With more than 200 homes on the lake, there were plenty of customers willing to pay a bit extra for the young man to cruise up to their dock with their dinner. Boaters on the lake also enjoyed the convenience of a hot meal delivered wherever they anchored. "They think it's an awesome summer job that I get to ride my jet ski around for a living and

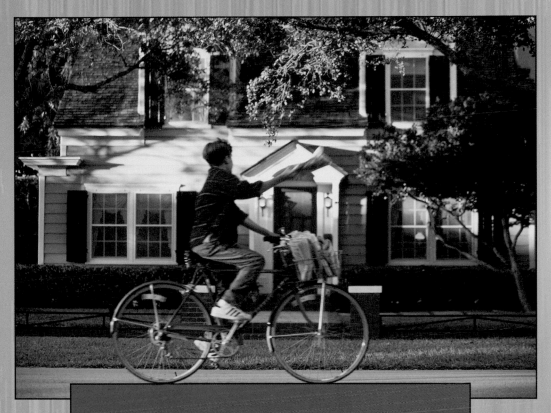

Delivering newspapers is one way to make money and be outside. There are many more!

it's good for them too," said Emerson. His hours are 5:00 until sunset, hours he spends out on the water, with the wind in his hair—all while getting paid! Emerson has no complaints: "I get to be on a jet ski all the time. I get to fly."

Of course, not everyone has a lake and a jet ski at their disposal. But Emerson is just one of many teens who have managed to turn their love of the great outdoors into a profitable venture. So, if you like hiking and biking or shooting hoops at the park best, think beyond four walls when you consider getting a job. All you need is hard work, determination, and a little imagination.

You may be wondering how to get started. There are plenty of options available for people who want to feel the sun (or snow) on their face as they earn their pay. In the next six chapters, you will explore the many outside jobs available to young people, whether you just need summer work or you're looking to start a career out of high school or college. Discover how to match up your skills and interests with the needs of your community and create your own opportunities. As you read, you'll be inspired by the stories of other young people just like you who have managed to earn a paycheck and enjoy nature at the same time.

Working for the Summer

Each year, as summer approaches, you start to dream about the day that books and homework will be replaced by sun and sleep. You've certainly earned a break! You want nothing more than to kick back poolside or in a backyard hammock and laze the days away.

But wait! There is a glitch in your plans. Maybe your parents want you do something more productive with your time. Or maybe you need cash to buy your first car. Don't worry! All is not lost. You can get yourself a summer job. Not in a stuffy office, but out in the fresh air. There are lots of jobs available during the summer months, and they have more perks than you might imagine. Not only can you soak up the sun as you earn your paycheck, but you can also learn new skills and meet some cool new people. Best of all, you might just find something that you really love doing and can turn it into a career down the road.

It's tempting to kick back and do nothing all summer. But getting a job has a lot more benefits in the long run.

Summer Job? No Sweat!

Seasonal work, which typically starts right around Memorial Day and runs through Labor Day, can be the perfect first job for a teen. This work is often available right in your hometown, depending on where you live. Do tourists commonly travel to your city, for example? Do you have amusement parks, natural scenic spots, or other attractions? These places often require extra help during the summer months. Other establishments in your city might have additional job openings during the summer, too. Jeff Allen, cofounder of Aboutjobs.com, told Katie Thomason of eHow, "Many year-round retail establishments have increased demand in the summer from increased tourism; restaurants might have expanded outdoor seating, and some stores have extended hours and need more staff."

Be sure also to look for potential jobs beyond your city or town. What attractions, resorts, or tourist spots can you find throughout your state? Don't stop there! Look online at job openings across the country, and then keep going—explore your options in other countries. Worldwide travel can be an amazing experience. Many reputable organizations offer jobs, accommodations, and travel expenses to teens willing to travel abroad for meaningful work. Some of the most common seasonal jobs include working at:

- Day or resident summer camps
- Amusement parks
- Holiday resorts and spas
- Tourist attractions

Becoming a camp counselor is a great idea if you love kids and love to spend time outside.

- Ranches and farms
- Tree and plant nurseries and landscaping services
- Sporting events
- Beaches
- City, state, and national parks
- Golf courses
- Agricultural farms
- Construction sites

Let's Get Started

If you decide that working a seasonal job sounds like fun, there are some important tips to remember. First, do your homework. Research what options you have and what kind of skills are required for each job. It is a waste of your time—and your potential employer's—to apply for a job that requires a certain skill set or certification that you don't actually have. Also, look into travel arrangements and costs. If you're working locally, your travel costs are going to be minimal, but if you have to fly to Europe, the cost can be quite substantial. Explore what the job does and does not offer. For example, if you have to live away from home while working, are food and accommodations provided, are they part of your payment, or will you have to pay for them yourself, out of your own pocket?

Second, be prepared to work long hours and many days in a row. For example, if you decide to spend the summer doing agricultural work like picking fruit, you will most likely work from dawn to dusk, though this pace may last only for a short period, such as one to two weeks. Being in good physical shape is essential—for this job and almost every type of outdoor work. A number of these positions will require you to use muscles you didn't

Jobs like gardening offer lots of sunshine and exercise, but also plenty of hard work.

know you had. And, in the beginning, each one of those muscles is sure to complain.

Third, be flexible in what kind of work you are willing to do when you are originally hired. In order to get your foot in the door of an organization or company, you might initially have to let go of the idea of working outside. Instead, you may begin to work your way up the ladder by laboring in the kitchen washing dishes, in the laundry room cleaning clothes, or even behind the snack bar serving drinks and nachos. You may also find yourself doing work you hadn't imagined. Working as a camp counselor, for example, might include teaching crafts and leading night hikes. But it also might require mending tents; cleaning out cabins, dining halls, and latrines; and handling plumbing problems.

Fourth, plan ahead. If you are applying for summer work, don't wait until May to start looking for a job. Experts suggest that you start in late winter or early spring. "As each day passes by, there will be less opportunity," Heather Boyer, director of marketing for SnagAJob.com, told Katie Thomason of eHow. Allen adds, "Application deadlines vary, but if you want a particular type of job with a specific employer, do your research now to find out when their application deadlines close so that you don't miss out on the opportunity."

Fifth, do some research regarding the job outlook for the field you are investigating. For example, for recreation workers, according to the *Occupational Outlook Handbook*, published by the Bureau of Labor Statistics, states that the median pay for this type of job is $11.80 per hour. The field is growing at an average rate of 9 percent, or about the same rate as the overall national average. Figure out how much you will make with this job. It should be minimum wage or better, unless money is taken out for food and lodging.

Finally, create a strong résumé that you can hand out, mail, email, or post in response to job listings. Make sure to include any of your skills, certifications, abilities, training, and professional experience on the résumé. Also ask for letters of recommendation or references from teachers and guidance counselors, former bosses and coworkers,

Lifeguarding, a great summer job that comes with lots of responsibility, requires training and certification.

and family friends. If you can speak more than one language, be sure to mention that. Also include extracurricular activities and volunteer positions.

The summer can be a wonderful opportunity to take a seasonal job. Make the most of those weeks by learning and earning!

YOUR FIRST RÉSUMÉ

At the entry level, many employers will simply ask you to fill out an application form. But in some cases, you will need to submit a résumé. Don't be intimidated! If you do a little research first, writing your first résumé is not an impossible task. Here are some things to keep in mind:

- You do not have to craft a résumé out of thin air. There are hundreds of books and lots of websites that contain examples of résumés. Search for entry-level or no-experience-required positions. Take note of the format and content of those résumés and then create one that is similar, but personalized for you.

- Start out with a summary. Write a few lines that explain why you would be great for this job. Are you reliable? energetic? creative? Say it. Now is not the time to be modest. Make sure you take

(continued on the next page)

(continued from the previous page)

into consideration the qualities the employer is likely to be looking for in an employee.

- Most employers hiring teens understand that you won't have lots of relevant work experience. That doesn't mean you don't bring anything to the table. You have life experience! Include sports, school accomplishments, clubs, activities, hobbies, and after-school jobs like babysitting or mowing lawns. All of these require skills that could transfer to the job you are seeking.

- Proofread! Look your résumé over for any grammar or spelling issues. Then have someone else, preferably an adult, read it. There should be no typos or misspellings in a résumé.

Beyond the Classroom

Imagine putting together your class schedule and having to choose between mountaineering, rock climbing, and wilderness medical school. If you're enrolled at National Outdoor Leadership School (NOLS), those just might be your options.

NOLS was established in 1965 and at first offered just three wilderness courses. One hundred young men showed up to enroll. In 1967, young women

Be ready for some serious adventure if you attend National Outdoor Leadership School.

were allowed to enroll, and by 1970, NOLS had more than 750 students. In the years since then, the organization has continued to expand, offering additional classes in more and more parts of the world. It is listed as the largest backcountry permit holder in the country. It has produced more than 250,000 graduates, has locations across the globe, and offers more than one hundred courses. For a number of years, NOLS has been listed as one of America's best places to work in *Outside Magazine*.

"NOLS exists to take people outside," Bruce Palmer, director of admissions and marketing, said. "We focus on leadership, environmental skills, and training people to be outdoor leaders. Courses run from ten days to seventy-seven days, but the average class is one month long." Every course NOLS offers to participants earns them college credit with the University of Utah.

The skills NOLS looks for in its leaders include advanced technical skills in one of the main sports (rock climbing, kayaking, skiing, etc.). Leadership candidates must also demonstrate strong communication skills and the ability to teach, plan, and expedite a course. Navigation skills are essential as well, including GPS, mapping, and compass use. Basic skills are also a priority, such as setting up a campsite and "leave no trace" camping practices. Palmer suggests that anyone who likes the outdoors and might want to pursue working for NOLS get as much experience as possible. "Join Boy Scout or Girl Scout troops that go camping," he said. "Anything that gets you outdoors is great."

You're In Charge

Do you have the spirit of an entrepreneur? You may want to consider striking out on your own. But first, a word of caution: the decision to start your own business should not be made lightly. While being your own boss may sound tempting, it's not for everyone. You need to ask yourself some questions and be honest with your answers. Are you responsible? Do you have lots of energy? Are you a self-starter? Do you have very specific ideas about what you would like to do for a job? If you answered "Yes!" to these questions, then starting a business may be the right path for you. Being your own boss

Jobs as basic as taking out the trash or shoveling snow can be the basis for your own company.

gives you the freedom to select only the work you want, to set your own hours and fees, and to not answer to anyone but yourself. On the flip side, it's a lot of responsibility riding on you alone. So let's take a closer look at what it takes to start a small business from the ground up.

Hit the Pavement

Liam and his family moved to Oregon a few months ago. Moving is a familiar process for all of them. At only fourteen years old, Liam has already lived in Arizona, California, Michigan, and Illinois. Since his family was often struggling to make ends meet, when Liam wanted to join Boy Scouts, the money just wasn't there. "He joined Scouts around his sixth birthday," his mother, Kathleen, remembered. Liam paid his own way by becoming one of the top five popcorn sellers in the entire district. He sold enough to cover the cost of his uniforms, fees, gear, and even summer camp.

"Next, he started brainstorming," said Kathleen. Liam was too young to babysit or walk dogs, but he was determined to do something to earn money and help out his family. "I made up business cards and fliers on the computer for my business, 'Just Ask Liam,'" he explained, "and I offered to take people's trash cans out to the curb the night before trash collection for $1." As he got older, Liam discovered other ways to make money in whatever neighborhood his family was currently living. One area had a lot of older residents, so he took in their groceries, weeded their gardens, and shoveled snow from their driveways. "I recycled for the neighborhood, too," added Liam. "I would go to people's houses and collect their aluminum and other recyclables, and then turn them in for whatever money I could get."

At eight, Liam took first aid and lifesaving courses with the Red Cross. "I did that for a few reasons," he explained. "It was part of earning a Boy Scout badge, plus I tend to be a bit accident-prone, so it was for my own benefit, too." He was hired as a mother's helper for some busy moms and also helped a woman with a feral cat program she was organizing. "I helped her catch the cats and feed them," Liam said. "I also helped make beds for the cats and prepare the shelter for the winter months." By this time, Liam was making at least $30 a week and over $100 a week in the spring.

Each time Liam's family moved, he would walk through his new neighborhood and "scope out the area." "I would look at the houses and see what people might need," he explained. "What services do they need done, but don't want to do? If you figure

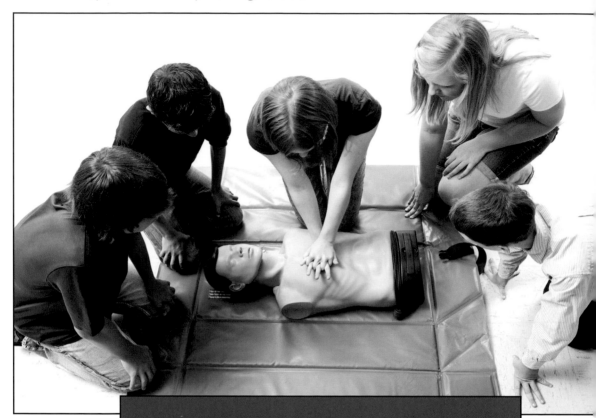

Taking CPR and first aid courses will teach you skills that you can use in any kind of business.

that out, find out the going rate for those services, and then charge slightly less, you will find work." Over the years, Liam has helped with construction, hauled trash to Dumpsters, walked dogs, watched children, and worked at local market booths on weekends. "He doesn't like making less than $40 a week," said Kathleen. "He just received a new batch of business cards and is about to start handing them out everywhere he can!"

Liam doesn't plan to work outside all of his life; he has plans to go to a culinary academy and become a combination chef and personal fitness trainer. In the meantime, he is learning skills, meeting people, earning money, and enjoying the outdoors—not a bad combination for an industrious fourteen-year-old!

Who Needs Help?

If you want to start your own business and become an entrepreneur like Liam, a great place to start is exploring the area where you live to see what services might be needed. If you are surrounded by apartment buildings, lawn care might not be the best choice. If you live in the South, snow shoveling is probably out of the question. If you have retirement homes or senior care facilities on either side, babysitting is not a likely option. What do you think the people around you might need the most?

Some of the most common types of self-employment jobs for young people include:

- Washing cars
- Mowing lawns

You can start a business offering services that are demand in your neighborhood, like washing cars.

- Doing yard work
- Babysitting children
- Walking pets
- Making repairs
- Holding yard sales
- Teaching outdoor skills
- Coaching sports
- Tuning bicycles

- Assisting with birthday parties
- Being a golf caddy
- Delivering newspapers
- Manning local market booths
- Weeding and watering gardens
- Lifeguarding at local pools, lakes, etc.
- Working at a day camp
- Selling home party supplies
- Delivering messages or documents by bicycle or on foot

As you look through this list or one you come up with yourself, ask yourself the following questions:

1. **Which of these services do I think would fit in best with the area where I live?** Look at the houses in the neighborhood—do any need lawn services? Pool care? Painting?

2. **What skills do these jobs require? Do they require skills that I already have, or do I need to learn something additional? If I do, where can I find classes, workshops, or internships to teach me these skills?** If you are competent at a skill, teaching it to others is wonderful, but be sure not to oversell yourself. Just because you beat your dad at chess every night does not

mean you are able to teach young people how to win chess competitions. If you attended a day camp last summer, you are not necessarily prepared and qualified to be a counselor this summer.

3. **How can I demonstrate to potential clients that I am professional and reliable? What certifications or training should I have to show to them?** If you are certified in first aid, for example, carry the card on you to show to potential customers. If you have earned a food handler's card, put it in your wallet to show you've done your homework!

4. **How much time do I want to dedicate to this job? How many hours per day and which days? Weekdays and/or weekends?** Remember, you will have to work around school hours, extracurricular requirements, and family obligations.

5. **Do I need any kind of insurance coverage for the jobs I am offering? If so, where do I find it?** Talk to your parents or a lawyer about whether or not you need to provide insurance coverage for the job you want to

When advertising your new business, consider using social media or a website to spread the word.

begin. If you're going to coach children's tennis, for example, what happens if someone gets hurt? You will need to know what insurance coverage exists and what you are legally required to carry.

6. **What kind of marketing and promotion do I need to do? Will I need flyers and business cards? If so, can I make them myself? Where should I post them? Should I use digital and**

social media to advertise my services? Ask family and friends to help get the word out by handing out printed materials and forwarding and posting digital ad content. Nowadays, many neighborhoods have online message boards—they are a great way to reach people in your area. Check with local merchants, as they are often open to promoting small businesses (just make sure your service isn't in competition with theirs). Post fliers on supermarket, public library, or town hall bulletin boards, town center kiosks, and other places where people stop and look.

Answering all of these questions carefully and thoroughly is a vital part of your business plan. If you want your particular service—whether it is mowing lawns or washing cars—to become an actual business, and not just something you do here and there as a hobby in order to make a few bucks, then you need to design a workable business plan. Being an entrepreneur is fun—but demanding. No one else is going to promote or advertise your services. It is up to you to network and reach out to people in a professional way. Remember that the impression you make on people with the way you speak, look, and behave is going to help sway them

A GENERATION OF ENTREPRENEURS

If you're thinking about starting your own business, you are not alone. According to one study, more than 40 percent of people born after 1996 plan to become entrepreneurs. Why? Today's teens and young adults have seen the effects of recession and student loan debt, and they're determined to be smart about money. Being your own boss is a great way to make money while doing something that is meaningful to you. And starting a small business while you're in high school not only boosts your chances of admission to the college of your choice, but you'll also be able to reduce student debt if you've been saving your paychecks. So, go ahead—start the business you've been dreaming of. You're in good company!

to hire you—or to look elsewhere. So talk, dress, and act responsibly!

Teen Success Stories

Creating your own business may sound exciting—and intimidating. Here are three young women who rose to the challenge.

Walking dogs is a business that could easily spread by word of mouth. If you do a good job with one dog, soon you may be walking a whole pack!

Madison (age fifteen) was inspired to start working for the same reason many people are—she wanted the money to buy something. In her case, it was a camera because she is interested in photography. She also likes dogs, so she started advertising a dog-walking business. She posted fliers throughout her neighborhood and waited. Finally, a woman called and asked Madison to walk Harley, a golden retriever. Madison enjoyed being with the dog and earning money, but walking in the rain and mud wasn't as much fun. "Working outside has taught me that I do not want to sit in an office all day long," Madison said. "The job has also taught me the importance of wearing good shoes and being truthful." Currently, she is searching for a few more dogs to join Harley.

Kaylee (fourteen) said that she loves being outside and found the perfect training ground and workplace through Trackers Earth, a school that teaches survival skills and arts. She took a class with them, became a teaching assistant, and then a counselor-in-training. "We are like a family that works together to take care of all aspects of our daily life, while teaching kids how to fish, build fires, weave baskets, cook on a rocket stove outdoors, gather wild edibles, carve wood with knives, and sneak silently through the woods," Kaylee explained. "My love of wild things and the willingness of the staff to teach me what they knew inspired me to join. Trackers is my second family. They encourage and coach me to grow and develop as, hopefully, a future staff member."

During her experience with Trackers, Kaylee has learned a great deal. "I've learned to bring up a fire from a mere coal, to sit still and quiet in the woods, listening to the calls of the birds to tell me if someone is near," she said. "I've learned how to hide myself, to remain completely unseen in the shadows. I've learned to weave and spin … I have developed a repertoire of survival skills that make me feel confident in going out in the wild." Kaylee hopes to keep working with kids. In the meantime, she advises other young people who want to work outdoors to start by overcoming adversity. "To become an outdoor teacher, you have to release your death grip on the modern world. Nobody can stay inside forever … Being an outdoor teacher gets your creative juices flowing and more learning takes place!"

Livia (sixteen) started providing henna tattoos to summer campers in Idaho. When camp was over, she came home, bought a kit, and started practicing on anyone who would sit still. Finally, she became a vendor at her city's farmers' market. "At that point,

I just wanted to be able to cover the cost of renting the space, and anything above that was just icing on the cake," Livia explained to the author. "I was in it for the experience and the fun, not to make money." The henna went well—soon she was being called to do parties and other events. Knowing what to charge was challenging, so Livia researched pricing online and went to other area markets to see what artists were charging. "You have to be really persistent, as there have been days where I only net $4, and other times where I net $150," she explained. "It's always hard to predict whether I'll be busy on market day, because it depends on the weather, if people are on vacation, and countless other factors that I'm not aware of and are unpredictable."

Although henna can be done indoors, Livia definitely prefers outdoors. "At the market, it is noisy and sunny and windy, and there's more of a festive atmosphere, which just makes it generally more enjoyable." Has working at the market changed how Livia sees her future? "Doing tattoos has shown me how to go through the process of applying for something, as well as making a résumé, and negotiating business with people who are always much older than me," she said.

Outdoor Intern

There are lots of ways to learn a new skill. Suppose you want to learn how to make birdhouses. You could take a book out of the library and read up on the subject. Or, you could go online and find websites with videos showing how to make a birdhouse. Both of these choices are good first steps in learning your new craft. But if you truly want to become an expert birdhouse builder, you want to find someone who knows how it's done. You want to talk to a professional, watch them at work, help them with small tasks, and ask lots of questions. Now you have the knowledge and tools you need to build that birdhouse.

Often, a hands-on approach is the most effective way to learn a skill. The same idea applies when you're thinking about getting a job in an area that interests you: An internship or apprenticeship might be just what you need to get started in that field. Many outdoor jobs offer opportunities to work as a trainee, providing valuable, on-the-job experience.

During your summer months, give some thought to applying to an internship program. It gives you a chance to learn a profession up close. You are able to

Working as a trainee or intern is one of the best ways to get valuable experience and find out if a job is right for you.

ask questions and explore different career avenues. In some cases, you might even get paid. Internships also allow you to network with people working within the field that interests you. They give you the chance to find out if the job you had imagined is anything like the reality of the day-to-day work.

Trainees Wanted

Some of the outdoor jobs that are frequently held by young interns (and that can eventually develop into careers) include:

- Construction workers
- Pest control workers
- Brick masons
- Fishery workers
- Carpenters
- Roofers
- Welders

Finding a place to work as an intern may be as easy as asking your mom or dad to look into the teen job opportunities where they work, exploring options with your guidance counselor, or talking to your neighbors and family friends. Other times, you may have to apply for an internship, which traditionally includes submitting a résumé and being interviewed. You should give each one of these steps the same focus and thoroughness that you would those of any other job application process.

Internships come in all sizes and shapes. They typically last for two to three months. If you're not sure where to start when exploring this employment avenue, check out the "Internship Predictor" at Internships.com. It can help you tailor your interests and preferences to the internships that are available. You can also search online to see what is available. When you do, be sure to put in the most precise search words you can (e.g., "communication internships" will not be as helpful as "student summer publishing internship Seattle Washington"). Some internships are paid, offering hourly or weekly wages or a stipend. Other internships are unpaid. It is often the case that the most popular fields and industries—such as television, film, fashion, magazine publishing, and communications/public relations—are unpaid. This is because there are so many young people willing to work for free

On-the-job training allows you to learn as you work and benefit from the knowledge and experience of a professional in the field.

in these industries while gaining valuable professional experience and networking opportunities. Some unpaid internships, however, may offer course credit for school. It is up to you to research these issues, and if you can't find the answer, ask! After all, asking questions to discover answers is what internships are all about.

ACE THAT INTERVIEW!

You submitted a fantastic résumé or job application, and you've been invited to come in for an interview. Great! Now it's time to prepare. Here are some top tips to make sure you make a positive impression in your interview:

Look the part. No matter what field the internship or job may be in, always look presentable. When in doubt, it is better to be overdressed (it shows you care about the interview) than underdressed.

Show up a few minutes early. Being five or ten minutes early shows your prospective employer that you are punctual and reliable. Do not be late!

Be prepared. Bring copies of your résumé, references, working papers, and identification.

Anticipate questions. Consult books or websites for typical interview questions and be ready with an answer. Focus on how you can be an asset to your employer, not just why the job would be good for you.

Have your own questions. Have a few prepared questions ready for the interviewer. It shows that you've given the job some thought and that you are prepared. Make sure you have several questions ready, because some of them may be answered during the course of the interview.

Make a connection. It sounds simple, but give a firm handshake and look the interviewer in the eye. Having strong interpersonal skills is an asset in most jobs.

Don't forget to say thank you. It's always a good idea to send a brief note (email or paper) thanking the interviewer for taking the time to meet with you.

A Permanent Position

Dimitri (age twenty-three) knew that he wanted a job that would allow him to make money, did not involve a desk, and made it possible to travel around and see the world. He discovered it through welding. After earning his two-year degree in welding, Dimitri was hired as a welder/fitter and was taught advanced skills and techniques while on the job. This position is much like a traditional paid internship.

Learning to weld has been challenging. According to Dimitri, the most difficult part is "learning to stand like a statue and move with vegetable slowness and mechanical precision. Some welds can be ruined if you breathe wrong," he explained. "Only surgeons have steadier hands than ours." Dimitri hopes to follow his welding internship with a stint working on ships at sea. "I simply like ships," he said. "Building ships and maybe being part of the onboard maintenance crew would be so rewarding."

In the meantime, Dimitri has some advice for other young people. "Be a good judge of your comfort zones," he said. "Working in a shop pays less than working in the field, but think about wearing heavy, protective clothing and working over metal that radiates heat like an oven under the summer sun. Also, be versatile—the more you can do, the

If you enjoy your internship and do a great job, it could lead to a full-time job.

more you are worth, and the more fun you can have. Finally, be safe—do what it takes to go home with all your extremities, even if it means going home without the job."

Step Up and Volunteer

Chances are that you picked up this book because you are looking to make money by getting a job. But there is another avenue you can take: becoming a volunteer. While you may not receive a paycheck, there are plenty of other rewards that go along with volunteering. Take a moment to consider all of the opportunities—personal, professional, and social—that open up to you when you give your time to help others.

Teen volunteering is popular throughout the country. According to the Bureau of Labor Statistics, more than a quarter of all sixteen- to nineteen-year-olds volunteer in some way. Why do so many teenagers give up their free time and opportunities to make money in order to volunteer instead? In addition to being motivated by compassion and a desire to help their community, these teens have also realized that volunteering gives them the chance to acquire many personal and professional advantages. Let's explore a few of them. Volunteering can:

Volunteering to help in your community allows you to make a real difference while exploring your job options.

- Give you valuable work experience that future employers will respect
- Help you learn to work with other people and be a part of a team
- Connect you with people and organizations that you might network with and/or work for in the future
- Introduce you to new careers you hadn't considered before

- Demonstrate which jobs you enjoy and which you don't
- Teach you skills like decision making and time management
- Enhance your résumé for future jobs and your application for college admissions and/or scholarships

Finding the Right Place

OK—you're sold! The idea of volunteering appeals to you and you recognize all the opportunities it might bring. The next step is figuring out what kind of volunteer work you wish to provide and for what kind of organization. Here are some resources to help zero in on your ideal volunteer position. Many of these can involve at least some outdoor work. Start by looking locally. You can talk with your guidance counselor or other staff at school to see if they are aware of volunteer requests. Some of the organizations that often seek young volunteers include:

- Nursing homes (reading out loud, leading games)
- Senior centers (teaching computer skills)

- City parks (clean up or trail building)
- Community gardens and nurseries (weeding, watering)
- Boys' Club or Girls' Club (helping with homework, leading games)
- City tour groups (showing city sites, answering questions)
- Museums and aquariums (helping with displays, leading tours, staffing the gift shop)
- Churches (teaching, cleaning, babysitting)
- Hospitals (delivering flowers, working in the gift shop)
- Public libraries (summer reading and literacy programs, storytelling)
- Performing arts theaters (ushering, helping with props and scenery)
- Community centers and local YMCAs (teaching classes, coaching, leading field trips)
- Animal shelters (walking dogs, cleaning cages and kennels)
- Local cable access stations (running errands)
- Recycling centers or thrift stores (organizing donations, taking payments)
- Local day camps (helping with games and other activities)
- Public and private schools (tutoring)

Find an organization that provides tours of an area of interest, whether it's a city, park, or museum. Volunteers are often trained to lead tours.

A number of local organizations often need volunteers. Check out the local branch of the Red Cross, for example. Check to see if your area has a search and rescue team. Go online to visit Habitat for Humanity and see if there are any projects planned in your area.

Draft a résumé and then go to these organizations in person. You may be asked to drop off your

LET'S GO TO THE ZOO!

Do you love all creatures, large and small? Then the zoo may be the place for you! Many zoos offer volunteer opportunities especially tailored to teens. Imagine spending your days outdoors, working around all sorts of cool animals. You get to go behind the scenes at the zoo, learning about the people who work there, the animals themselves, their habitats, and conservation efforts. You may also act as a liaison between the zoo and the public, providing information and answering questions, so you'd be gaining valuable "people skills" to apply to future jobs. If hanging around lions, tigers, and bears sounds like your dream volunteer job, check out the zoo nearest you.

information or schedule a time for a face-to-face interview. Of course, you should also be ready to explain why you want to volunteer. You should genuinely believe in and be committed to the work being done by the organization for which you hope to volunteer. The services that these organizations provide are so important that they don't want to take on teens whose only interest in the work is to polish their college applications and résumés.

Volunteering with a search and rescue team usually requires training, but it can be extremely rewarding.

Make a Real Difference

Imagine searching the base of a mountain, along darkened trails, or through dense forest for a hiker who is missing. If you are part of a search and rescue (SAR) team, that might be exactly what you're doing. A number of SAR teams rely on teen volunteers to help them when a person goes missing. Coogan (age sixteen) joined SAR a year ago and fell in love with it. "It's hard and tiring and exhausting, but I still love it," he said. "Ninety-nine percent of the time we are outside, and it is cold and wet, but I love working outside. It is one of the best places to be."

Through his training with SAR, Coogan has learned how to perform first aid and CPR, use a portable defibrillator (a device that can normalize the rhythm of a human heart in emergency situations). He has been trained to navigate by compass or map; construct a shelter that can withstand rain, wind, and snow; and build a fire that can burn all night. "I have also learned not to lean against small trees— they might fall," he said. "Also, listen. If you don't listen to your teammates, you or someone else could get injured."

When his time with SAR is over, Coogan is planning on joining fire and rescue. For other young people who might be interested in joining their local SAR team, Coogan has some advice. "Be prepared—this isn't easy—it is hard work. Know that when you are out there on a search, you are saving someone's life, not goofing off with friends. If you choose to join SAR, I want you to be prepared to have some of the best years of your life," he added. "You'll make friends fast, and they will help you through it all."

Building Homes, Helping People

Ever since 1976, Habitat for Humanity (H4H), a nonprofit organization, has helped build more than 800,000 homes across the country. This group depends largely on volunteers for its outdoor projects and offers programs for young children, teenagers, and young adults. One volunteer, Nicole (age twenty-one), saw H4H as offering the perfect combination to satisfy her passion for both the outdoors and for hard and meaningful work. "My parents told me over and over again that the best way to get a job is to volunteer first," she said. "So, I strapped on a tool belt, bought my own hammer to make me feel official, and walked onto my first H4H construction site."

The work was far from easy. "Crawling underneath a house with a ventilator over your mouth and goggles over your eyes to install insulation with a nail gun is NOT fun," she admitted. What was fun for Nicole, however, was working outside and being part of a team. "I'm a sucker for camaraderie," she explained. "No matter how hard the work is, if you've got people who are laughing, joking, and suffering along with you, the job is nothing. Habitat gives you a glimpse of people trusting you in an age where you aren't always given trust. For me, it was a chance to prove myself TO myself."

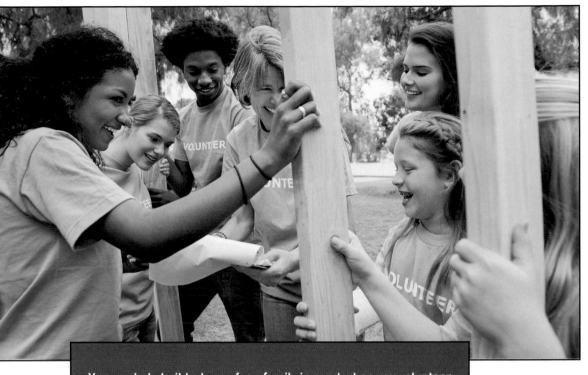

You can help build a home for a family in need when you volunteer with Habitat for Humanity.

After her time with H4H, Nicole went on to two years in search and rescue, and then to six months working on a tourist train in Alaska. Next, she led field trips for a local community center. Currently, she is preparing for a six-month exploration of the exotic Australian Outback. She hopes all young people know that working outdoors may not be easy, but it is always worth it. "What helps is having a goal," she said. "Traveling is what I want to do and what I want to BE. When you have a dream as fierce as that, everything else is small fish!"

Getting Down to Business

You might think that the hard work is over when you find your ideal outdoor job. Not so fast! There is a lot to know and think about before (and after) you agree to start work. As a teenager, how many hours are you allowed to work? What will you be paid? Will you have to file a tax return? Along with getting a job, there are laws to be considered, paperwork to fill out, and records to keep. But don't worry. There are plenty of resources to help you along the way.

You might recall from history classes that long ago, there were no laws regarding how many hours or what kinds of jobs minors could have. That might sound like a lot of freedom, but it was just the opposite. Until child labor laws were developed, even very young children could be put to work for forty hours or more a week. It was a cruel practice that severely harmed a lot of young people, so the government stepped in and developed some guidelines. How do they apply to you today?

STAY SAFE!

Today's laws go a long way to keep young people safe in the workplace, both physically and emotionally. Your employer should be familiar with all of the rules and regulations that are in place to ensure that employees do not get injured or sick on the job. But you should also be aware of those safety requirements and make sure they're being followed. The following areas are key to safety in the workplace:

Training—You should receive proper training before starting any job. This will ensure that you do everything according to the rules and don't risk injury.

Supervision—There should always be a supervisor present when you are working. In the event of an accident, report to the supervisor.

Equipment—Any equipment that you use should be in good working order. If you notice anything is broken or not working correctly, speak to your supervisor.

Health—Your health should be your first concern. If, for example, you are working outside for long periods of time, you should have regular breaks, particularly on hot days. Get in the shade and drink water. These breaks should be agreed upon with your employer.

(continued on the next page)

(continued from the previous page)

Stress—Most jobs come with a certain level of stress. But if you are made to feel uncomfortable or feel that the conditions in your workplace are unreasonably stressful, speak up.

Today's child labor laws are designed to strike a balance between the interests and desires of industrious teens and the necessary protections that will prevent exploitation of young workers. Careful limits are placed on the amount of hours teens can work on what days and in what times of the year, the types of workplace, and the working conditions. All of this is meant to protect the freedoms of teens who wish to work while helping to guarantee that that work will be safe and gratifying, will pay fairly, and will not infringe upon or detract from their schooling.

Who Is Allowed to Work?

Where and how much you can work is based on three main factors: your age, if school is in session, and how dangerous the work is. Federal child labor laws outline what age you must be to do certain kinds of jobs. Take a look at the chart of these general national guidelines on the next page and see which category fits you the best. Keep in mind that individual states also have their own rules about working.

AGE	HOURS PERMITTED	TYPES OF JOBS
Under 14 years old		Deliver newspapers Babysit Act/perform in movies, TV, or theater Family-owned business
14–15 years old	3 hours or less/school days 18 hours or less/week when school is in session 8 hours or less/day when school is out 40 hours or less/week when school is out Only between the hours 7 a.m. to 7 p.m. on any day except when school is out, and then it extends to 9 p.m.	Retail jobs Computer work Errands/delivery Pumping gas/washing cars Food service/limited cooking Lifeguarding/amusement parks Yard work without power-driven equipment
16–17 years old	No limitations	Any job that has not been declared hazardous* by the secretary of labor
18+ years old	No limitations	No limitations

*What qualifies as hazardous? According to the secretary of labor, anyone under the age of eighteen is banned from clearly dangerous actions and activities. This includes manufacturing/storing explosives, coal mining, using hazardous machines (like balers, compactors, or tools such as circular saws, chain saws, or wood chippers). If you're under eighteen, you will have to wait to get a job that involves these activities and equipment. You will also be excluded from jobs in demolition, roofing, or excavating.

Uncle Sam Takes His Cut

If you haven't heard the old adage yet, here it is:

The only inevitable parts of life are death and taxes. How much you will have to pay to the government each year depends on many factors. There is a strong chance that you will not owe anything. If you are listed as a dependent on your parents' taxes and earn less than the standard deduction in the previous year, for example, you don't have to file a tax return. (The standard deduction for 2018 was $12,000.) Make sure you note your exemption on the W-4 form provided by your employer.

Most jobs have a minimum age requirement. Be sure to check the laws in your area.

What if you have your own business though? You may need to pay federal income tax as well as self-employment tax. Carol Topp, an accountant and the founder of Teens and Taxes says that while there's a good chance you won't have to pay federal income tax, "if you make a profit of more than $400, you must pay self-employment."

Eve Davis, licensed tax consultant and president of In and Out Taxes in Portland, Oregon, agrees.

Do the math! If you have to pay taxes on your income, do some calculations to find out just how much you'll be paying.

"There are legal ramifications to not reporting your income. There is interest, plus penalties for late payments that can run as high as 50 percent of the self-employment tax," she explained. In addition, there is a penalty for not filing at all. "If you wait for more than three years," explained Davis, "even if you were due a refund, you won't be able to get it." Davis's bottom line advice is, "If your employer does not withhold any taxes, consult a tax professional. That way you will not make any mistakes that could later cost you money!"

If you are self-employed, it is essential that you remember to keep accurate, detailed records of how much you make and what business expenses and deductions (supplies, dues, equipment, advertising, etc.) you might require for your job. You will report this information on the IRS form Schedule C Profit and Loss Business form. When you are an entrepreneur with your own business, it can be a shock to discover that you have to pay self-employment tax. This tax takes a little over 15 percent of your profit.

Looking Ahead

With hard work and determination, you landed your outdoor job. You were able to spend your hours out in the sunshine, learning new skills and meeting interesting people. Perhaps you worked as a camp counselor or a gardener, or maybe you started your own lawn-mowing business. In any case, you've gained plenty of valuable experience and made important connections. You learned what it means to be responsible and work hard, and hopefully you benefitted, financially or in other ways.

So what comes next? What do you do with all of this work experience? Great questions! Answering, however, requires asking a few more questions.

Your job may turn out to be the first step toward a career, or just a good way to make money for now. Either way, you've gained valuable experience.

1. **Have you enjoyed all of the time you have spent outside?** This may seem like a silly question, but you may have discovered that being out in whatever conditions nature chooses to serve up—including everything from mosquitoes and humidity to frozen fingertips and bitter wind—is not the right career path for you. If you didn't like the experience, chances are you need to start looking in another direction, possibly indoors.

2. **If you started your own business, do you plan to continue it? The answer to this question probably depends on many factors: Did your business succeed? Did you enjoy it?** Is there an ongoing market for it? Do you have the time, energy, and desire to pursue it? If the answers are yes to these questions, you know where to look next. If the answers are no, it is time to investigate other options.

3. **Do you plan to go to college?** If the answer to this question is no, you need to decide how you want to funnel your passion for being outdoors into a job that does not require a college degree. This may involve additional internships or apprenticeships; some coursework at a trade,

Sit down with a guidance counselor or teacher, talk about your future career goals, and make a plan.

technical, or community college; or the creation of your own company. Blake Boles, author of *Better than College: How to Build a Successful Life Without a Four-Year Degree*, suggests that young people who aren't going to college instead pursue the concept of "self-directed learning." He explained to *HuffPost*, "Instead of taking full-time classes, self-directed learners give themselves assignments that they find interesting, eye-opening, and challenging. They start businesses, find internships, travel the world, read and write about things that fascinate them, and work for organizations they admire." If you do plan to go to college, however, you need to explore which colleges offer some of the best outdoor career options. You also must learn how to translate your outside work experience into a college and/or scholarship application that will get the attention of the admissions department.

Advice from the Pros

Gen and Kelly Tanabe are the founders of SuperCollege, as well as the authors of fourteen books, including *Get into Any College*. They are experts on how to apply for and receive college scholarships and believe that kids who work outdoors learn many essential skills. "Students who work outdoors learn myriad skills that would be applicable to college applications," Kelly Tanabe said. "They learn how to work independently, a skill that is necessary not only for completing the applications but also for succeeding in college. Unlike traditional jobs, outdoor jobs often offer students the ability to work on their own without

In college, you'll have the opportunity to take classes that prepare you for a career in your area of interest.

direct oversight from a manager. This encourages them to work independently," added Tanabe.

Students who spend time working outside also gain a hands-on understanding of the sciences, such as biology, chemistry, botany, and environmental science. "Certainly, students also learn creative problem solving because nature doesn't always behave the way that you think it would," Tanabe added. "Colleges seek students who have a passion for an area because they know that students will carry over this passion into their studies and future career." Tanabe believes that colleges appreciate students who show a respect for nature and environmentalism. "Colleges themselves are increasingly building green buildings and developing recycling programs, which means that they seek students who will contribute to their efforts," she stated.

"When students have an outdoor experience that they enjoy before college, it can help guide them to select a college that is an outdoors-oriented location," Tanabe went on to explain. "They may choose a college that allows them to hike, snowboard, or mountain bike over one that is an urban location. Students may also select a college that has an outdoors program. After their outdoors experience, students may find that they want to study an area that is related to the outdoors, which will also guide their college selection."

When asked what young people can possibly do to make the most of their outdoor experiences if they're going to college, Tanabe replied, "Students should try to hold as many responsibilities as possible, hold a leadership position if possible, and take initiative on projects. Leadership is a quality

THE RIGHT SCHOOL FOR YOU

Some colleges are great for outdoor enthusiasts simply because of where they are located. Others offer programs and degrees directly related to the outdoors—for example, at Warren Wilson College in North Carolina, you can major in Outdoor Leadership. Great Value Schools compiled a list of 50 of the best affordable schools for those who love the outdoors. Here are the top ten:

10. Warren Wilson College
9. University of Alaska Fairbanks
8. University of Utah
7. Boise State University
6. University of Colorado Boulder
5. University of Hawaii at Manoa
4. Appalachian State University
3. Middlebury College
2. Montana State University
1. University of California, Berkeley

that colleges seek in accepting students."

The time you spend under the sun and the stars will always be a part of your life. Whether you use it to pursue a full-time career, develop your own entrepreneurial company, have fun and foster hobbies—or you decide that you much prefer working inside four walls rather than outside them—it will not be time wasted. Mother Nature has a lot to offer, and you can find the best possible way to connect with her through an investment of time, persistence, and dedication.

Landing a Job

Wondering what it takes to get hired at a camp or other outdoor organization? According to Tony Deis, the founder of Trackers Earth in Oregon and California, it requires a great deal of time spent in the field. "Experience is—hands-down—what gets you hired," he said. "There are other important skills that you can develop, of course, but field experience is the key."

Trackers Earth was established in 2004 and is largely based on Deis's work with the Audubon Society of Portland, Metro Parks, Greenspaces, and Portland State University. Over the last fifteen years, Trackers Earth has become one of the largest and most successful summer camps and outdoor programs in Oregon. As Deis defines the organization, "Trackers Earth exists to re-create a village of people connected through family and the land. We lead the way in education and collaborative organization. Our method is to revive outdoor

Getting started in the workforce isn't easy, but once you gain experience, you'll be on your way to landing your dream job.

lore and traditional skills, working to restore the common sense that is no longer common." Deis also says, "Our vision is to help foster a keen appreciation for the natural world and community."

Each year, Trackers Earth receives thousands of applications. Of those, only a fraction are granted interviews, and even fewer are hired. Competition for a position with this organization is fierce.

"Working with Trackers Earth can either be the most satisfying or the most infuriating experience of your career," says Deis. "We don't run things in the conventional way. We have highly flexible and agile development schedules in order to work with very high standards. Trackers acts more like a family than a conventional business. We're often informal, sarcastic, geeky, and definitely intense." In addition to field experience and outdoor know-how, Deis hires people who demonstrate child and group management skills.

If working for an organization like Trackers Earth sounds like the perfect job, how can you start preparing for it? Many of these types of organizations require at least a year or more of experience in outdoor camps, so start by volunteering at local camps and check to see if they offer any local educator training programs.

GLOSSARY

accommodations Lodging, food, and travel-related services.

application A request or petition, as for a job; a form used to make such a request.

apprentice One who is learning—by practical experience and under skilled workers—a trade, art, or calling.

certification The process of being recognized as having met special qualifications (by a governmental agency or professional board) within a field.

deduction An act of taking away; something that is or may be subtracted.

dependent Someone who relies on another for support; not independent.

entrepreneur One who organizes, manages, and assumes the risks of a business or enterprise.

exploitation The act of using someone unfairly for personal gain.

extracurricular Not falling within the scope of a regular curriculum; of or relating to officially or semiofficially approved and usually organized student activities connected with school and usually carrying no academic credit.

field experience The practical, first-hand knowledge gained by doing a job.

internship A program in which an advanced student or graduate usually in a professional field gains supervised practical experience.

marketing The process of selling or promoting a product, person, or business.

median Average

networking The exchange of information or services among individuals, groups, or institutions; the cultivation of productive relationships for employment or business.

recommendation A positive endorsement of a person or product.

résumé A short account of one's career and qualifications prepared typically by an applicant for a position; a set of accomplishments.

retail Having to do with selling goods.

self-promotion The act of publicizing your positive traits and skills in order to get a job or other benefit.

stipend A fixed sum of money paid periodically for services or to defray expenses.

tax A percentage of income that is paid to the government.

venture An undertaking involving chance, risk, or danger; a speculative business enterprise.

volunteer A person who undertakes or expresses a willingness to undertake a service of his or her own free will and choice; to offer oneself as a volunteer.

FURTHER READING

Books

Burnette, Josh. *Adulting 101: #Wisdom4Life*. Savage, MN: Broadstreet, 2018.

Callahan, Meredith Whipple. *Indispensable: How to Succeed at Your First Job and Beyond*. Oakland, CA: Quill, 2018.

DK. *Heads Up Money*. New York, NY: DK, 2017.

Kallen, Stuart A. *Careers If You Like the Outdoors*. San Diego, CA: ReferencePoint Press, 2017.

Pigatt, Matthew A. *Academic Hustle: The Ultimate Game Plan for Scholarships, Internships, and Job Offers*. Coral Gables, FL: Mango, 2018.

Slomka, Beverly. *Teens and the Job Game*. Herndon, VA: Mascot Books, 2018.

Websites

CareerOneStop: GetMyFuture
www.careeronestop.org/GetMyFuture/default.aspx
Sponsored by the Department of Labor, this site is loaded with resources for finding a job, getting training, writing a résumé, and becoming your own boss.

IRS: Understanding Taxes – Student
apps.irs.gov/app/understandingTaxes/student/index.jsp
Learn the basics about taxes, including who has to
pay and how to file a return.

US Department of Labor: Youth and Labor
www.dol.gov/general/topic/youthlabor
Check out the information you need as a young
worker, including labor laws, age requirements,
wages, and work permits.

YouthRules! Everything You Need to Know to Work
www.youthrules.gov/index.htm
Provides government requirements for safety in
the workplace as well as lots of other resources
including a young worker toolkit.

BIBLIOGRAPHY

Boles, Blake. *Better Than College: How to Build a Successful Life Without a Four-Year Degree.* Springfield, OR: Tells Peak Press, 2012.

Boles, Blake. "How to Build a Successful Life Without a Four-Year Degree." Huffington Post College Blog, September 1, 2012. http://www.huffingtonpost.com/blake-boles/how-to-build-a-successful-life_b_1644107.html.

Bureau of Labor Statistics. "Recreation Workers." *Occupational Outlook Handbook.* April 13, 2018. https://www.bls.gov/ooh/personal-care-and-service/recreation-workers.htm.

D'Angelo, Bob. "Michigan teen starts jet ski food delivery service." Cox Media Group. July 29, 2017. https://myconnection.cox.com/article/nationalnews/d7629320-7423-11e7-803d-997225c646f7/

Davis, Eve. Interview with Tamra Orr for *Money-Making Opportunities for Teens Who Like Working Outside.* August 9, 2012.

Deis, Tony. Interview with Tamra Orr for *Money-Making Opportunities for Teens Who Like Working Outside.* August 8, 2012.

Devantier, Alecia T. *Extraordinary Jobs in Agriculture and Nature.* New York, NY: Ferguson, 2006.

Edwards, Dimitri. Interview with Tamra Orr for
*Money-Making Opportunities for Teens Who
Like Working Outside.* August 8, 2012.

Entrepreneur Staff. "41 Percent of Gen Z-ers
Plan to Become Entrepreneurs." *Entrepreneur.*
January 15, 2019. https://www.entrepreneur
.com/article/326354.

Finley, Ellen. Interview with Tamra Orr for *Money-
Making Opportunities for Teens Who Like
Working Outside.* August 5, 2012.

Fowler, Janet. "15 Great Summer Jobs for Teens."
Investopedia. May 12, 2017. https://www
.investopedia.com/financial-edge/0612/10-great
-summer-jobs-for-teens.aspx.

GVC Staff. "50 Great Affordable Colleges for
Outdoor Enthusiasts." Great Value Colleges.
January 2019. https://www.greatvaluecolleges
.net/affordable/outdoor-enthusiasts/

Hershman, Livia. Interview with Tamra Orr for
*Money-Making Opportunities for Teens Who
Like Working Outside.* August 6, 2012.

Karas, Elizabeth. Interview with Tamra Orr for
*Money-Making Opportunities for Teens Who
Like Working Outside.* August 9, 2012.

Keeler, Doris. "Benefits of Volunteering for Teens." Youth Development at Suite 101, February 23, 2009. http://suite101.com/article/benefits-of -volunteering-for-teens-a98091.

Kekacs, Madison. Interview with Tamra Orr for *Money-Making Opportunities for Teens Who Like Working Outside*. July 28, 2012.

Lyen, Kaylee. Interview with Tamra Orr for *Money-Making Opportunities for Teens Who Like Working Outside*. August 5, 2012.

Matteson, Coogan. Interview with Tamra Orr for *Money-Making Opportunities for Teens Who Like Working Outside*. August 4, 2012.

Misner, Ivan, and Michelle R. Donovan. *The 29% Solution: 52 Weekly Networking Success Strategies*. Austin, TX: Greenleaf Book Group Press, 2008.

Occupational Safety and Health Administration. "Hazards." United States Department of Labor. Retrieved April 5, 2019. https://www.osha.gov /youngworkers/hazards.html.

Orr, Caspian. Interview with Tamra Orr for *Money-Making Opportunities for Teens Who Like Working Outside*. August 4, 2012.

Orr, Nicole. Interview with Tamra Orr for *Money-Making Opportunities for Teens Who Like Working Outside*. July 29, 2012.

Palmer, Bruce. Interview with Tamra Orr for *Money-Making Opportunities for Teens Who Like Working Outside*. August 7, 2012

Sabitano, Colleen. "The Changing Role of the Intern." Internships.com. Retrieved April 5, 2019. http://www.internships.com/student/resources/basics/the-changing-role-of-the-intern.

Shepherd, Liam. Interview with Tamra Orr for *Money-Making Opportunities for Teens Who Like Working Outside*. August 6, 2012.

Tanabe, Gen, and Kelly Tenabe. Interview with Tamra Orr for *Money-Making Opportunities for Teens Who Like Working Outside*. August 10, 2012.

Thomason, Katie. "First Summer Jobs: Putting Your Teen to Work." eHow. Retrieved July 2012. http://www.ehow.co.uk/feature_8276856_first-jobs-putting-teen-work.html.

Topp, Carol. "Teenagers and Self-Employment Tax." Teens and Taxes. February 22, 2019. http://teensandtaxes.com/self-employment-tax-on-teenagers/.

Vacation Works. *Summer Jobs Worldwide 2012.*
    Richmond, England: Crimson Publishing, 2011.
"Volunteering in the United States, 2015." Bureau
    of Labor Statistic. February 25, 2016. https://
    www.bls.gov/news.release/volun.nr0.htm.
Von Borg, Jacob. Interview with Tamra Orr for
    *Money-Making Opportunities for Teens Who
    Like Working Outside.* August 3, 2012.

INDEX

A

accommodations, 9, 11
age requirements, 54–55
Allen, Jeff, 9, 13
American Red Cross, 21, 46
amusement parks and resorts, 9
animal and pet care, 21, 24, 45
applications, college, 44, 47, 62
applications, job, 13, 15, 36, 38, 67
apprenticeships, 34, 60
Asselta, Emerson, 4–5

B

babysitting, 16, 20, 21, 22, 23, 24, 45
Boles, Blake, 61–62
Boyer, Heather, 13
Boy Scouts, 18, 20–21
business cards, 20, 23, 27

C

camps, day, 9, 25–26, 45, 59, 68
camps, summer, 9, 20, 32, 66
certifications, 11, 14, 26
child labor laws, 52, 53, 54–56
coaching, 24, 27, 45
construction jobs, 10, 22, 36, 50
counseling, camp, 13, 26, 31, 59
counseling, guidance, 14, 36, 44
course credits, 18, 38

D

Davis, Eve, 57–58
Deis, Tony, 66–68
delivery services, 4, 25, 45
dog walking, 20, 22, 31, 45

E

entrepreneurs, 19, 23, 28, 29, 58, 66
extracurricular activities, 15, 16, 26

F

first aid and CPR, 21, 26, 49

G

gardening and yardwork, 21, 24, 25, 45, 59
Girl Scouts, 18
golf courses and caddying, 10, 25

H

Habitat for Humanity (H4H), 46, 50–51

I

internships, 25, 34, 35, 36–38, 40, 60, 62
interviews, 36, 38–39, 47, 67

L

landscaping, 10
laundry, 12–13
lawns, mowing, 16, 23, 25, 28, 59
leadership skills, 18, 64–65
letters of recommendation, 14, 39
lifeguards, 25

M

messenger services, 25

N

National Outdoor Leadership School (NOLS), 16–18
navigation skills, 18, 49
networking (making connections), 28, 35, 38, 43, 59
newspaper delivery, 25

O

on-the-job-training, 34–36
Outside Magazine, 18

P

Palmer, Bruce, 18
parks, 10, 45

R

recycling programs, 21, 45, 64
references, 14, 39
résumés, 14, 15–16, 33, 36, 38, 39, 44, 46, 47

S

safety, workplace, 41, 53, 54
search and rescue (SAR), 46, 48–49, 51
seasonal jobs, 8, 9, 11, 15
self-employment, 57–58
snow shoveling, 21, 23

T

Tanabe, Gen, 62
Tanabe, Kelly, 62–65
taxes, 52, 56–58
Thomason, Katie, 9, 13
Topp, Carol, 57
tourist attractions, 8, 9, 51
Trackers Earth, 31–32, 66–68
trash collection, 20–21, 22
travel expenses, 9, 11
tutoring, 45

V

volunteer work, 15, 42, 44, 46, 47, 48, 50, 68

W

washing cars, 23, 28
washing dishes, 12

Y

yard sales, 24